Independence Versus Conformity, Revisiting a Solomon E Asch Study: Psychology in Action

Independence Versus Conformity, Revisiting a Solomon E Asch Study: Psychology in Action

SGC

Steven G Carley

SGC Production

Boston, Massachusetts

Steven would grow-up in a small town in Boston, Massachusetts playing with other children in his neighborhood. Steven would lead a mostly quiet life spending much of his time devoted to his studies. Steven would view himself more as a curious person than as a genius. He was born on July 13, 1975, his father was a machinist and mother Beverly was daughter to a machinist. Steven liked running and climbing but most of all he liked collecting, match box cars, baseball cards, muscle men figures, and pretty much anything else he could get his hands on. Steven would grow-up with his two sisters who as mentioned earlier would lead a relatively quiet life.

Steven was not a very successful student during high-school and at times would rebel at home by sneaking out of the house at night to join in the endeavors of locals in the neighborhood. Despite Steven's lackluster performance in high-school he would succeed within University of Phoenix receiving a Bachelor of Science degree graduating with honors. During this time Steven would author four works pertaining to his area of study and another on the secrets to self-publishing. He may be most known for his collection of 60+ e-books. He is currently continuing his studies within the IO Psychology Ph.D. program in which he is hoping to complete his Master's degree by 2015 and Doctorate degree by 2018.

stevecarley.us

Contents

Independence Versus Conformity, Revisiting a Solomon E Asch Study: Psychology in Action

Independence Versus Conformity is a look back at the research of Solomon E Asch. At the time his work would be a successful attempt at supporting the earliest research pertaining to social psychology, the scientific study of how behavior can be affected by social surroundings. This research as it would turn would support the notion individual opinion could be easily altered the result of the opinions of one's social surrounding. Asch would take more of a hands-on approach within his demonstration as compared to the work of Bernheim, as an example. Asch's 1955 study would act as a middle ground, bridging the earliest studies of the beginning of the 20th century to the present day findings of a more modern social psychology. The research in creation of this report would act as a follow-up to the 1955 study, in a creative means of putting the author himself in an evaluatory position within the actual experiment.

Independence Versus Conformity, Revisiting a Solomon E Asch Study: Psychology in Action

In obtaining expressed permission from the work's author to use the material, a written request should be sent to SGC Production, Permissions Department, 19 Riley Rd. Suite 17, Boston, MA 02136 or email requests can be made through info@sgcproduction.com.

Among the times of publishing and gathering website information the closing of sites is not uncommon. Resulting in typographical errors can be the transcription of URLs. Where these errors occur the publisher would appreciate notification so in subsequent editions these errors may meet correction.

ISBN-13: 978-0615889979 ISBN-10: 0615889972

Independence Versus Conformity, Revisiting a Solomon E Asch Study: Psychology in Action

Steven G Carley

SGC Production

Print Edition

Independence Versus Conformity, Revisiting a Solomon E Asch Study: Psychology in Action

Psychology in Action Part I

"Psychology in Action Part I" involves an identification of the social psychology issues explored in Asch's study on social pressure and opinion. A description will occur of the researcher's theoretical approach to social behavior evidenced through the existing methodologies of his study. In addition will be an explanation of the methodology of the research within Asch's study and the appropriateness to his study. Finally, a discussion will occur of Asch's approach to the self and social conformity as expressed through his study on social pressure and individual opinion; furthermore, a biography of Solomon E. Asch will occur. Solomon Asch's work on opinion and social pressures is a true voyage into the science of social psychology.

Exploration into Solomon E Asch and His Conformity Study

Biography of Solomon P. Asch. Solomon Eliot Asch was born in Warsaw, Poland on September 14, 1907. He would die in Haverford, Pennsylvania, at the age of 88 on February, 20, 1996. Some of his selected major publications would include: Effects of group pressure upon the modification and distortion of judgment (1951), Opinions and social pressure (1955), Studies of independence and conformity: A minority of one against a unanimous majority (1956), and Social psychology (1987). At the age of 13 in 1920 Solomon's family would move to the United States. Solomon and his family would live in Manhattan in New York and through his reading of Charles Dickens Solomon would learn to speak the English language. Asch would attain a bachelor's degree in 1928 from the College of the City of New York. He would earn both his master's (1930) and Ph.D. (1932) from Columbia University where he would receive mentoring from Max Wertheimer (Cherry, 2013).

During Solomon's time as a professor in the psychology department at Brooklyn College, he would study the impact of propaganda and indoctrination. Asch would also work with Wolfgang Kohler while a professor at Swarthmore College where he would serve for 19 years. Asch would become famous during the 1950s for his Asch conformity experiments demonstrating how social pressures lead to conformity. As a professor at the Institute for Cognitive Studies at Rutgers University Asch would hold the title of both director and distinguished professor of psychology. Among both social and gestalt psychology Solomon Asch meets consideration as a pioneer. Even to the present-day Asch's conformity experiments are a source of inspiration for social psychology researchers demonstrating the power of social influence. Asch would not only supervise Stanley Milgram's Ph.D. at Harvard University but also act as the inspiration for his obedience research. Asch would believe people to act decently upon one another despite his work often depicting the negative influences of peer pressures on social behavior (Cherry, 2013).

Social Psychology Issues Within Asch's Study. Solomon Asch studies the effects of social influence on the individual. Social influence can affect individual beliefs, judgments, or practices. Personal opinion can become constrained by both group pressures and the existing social forces. As Asch would demonstrate through his experimental study opinion may be no more than a construction of social influence. Asch's studies would be a means of either strengthening early 20th century findings on similar experiments or conversely to find the experiments to possess manipulated statistics (Asch, 1955, p. 2). In Asch's study he shows two white cards with one line on one card and three lines on the other card of obvious varying sizes to a group of seven to nine college males. During the first two rounds each agree on the size of the line. During the next two rounds a lone dissenter is present. This individual is unaware the rest of the group receives instruction to provide the wrong response to test the effects of social influence on individual judgment. The unanimous majority increase the error rate among judgment by 35%, as the error response rate is less than one-percent and the individual through social influence sways toward the majority response providing the wrong answer 36.8% of the time (Asch, 1955, p. 3). This is of a group of 123 subjects. Asch would also test the effects of a non-unanimous majority and the effects of social influence within smaller groups of one or two. A group of one where one dissenter was present would result in the individual continuing to provide an independent response. A group of two dissenter's would increase the erroneous response rate to 13.6%. A unanimous dissenting group of three would provide a 31.8% error rate, and this rate would not significantly change if the group of dissenters would increase (Asch, 1955, p. 5). The presence of a partner against a dissenting group would diminish wrong responses to 25%, and whether the individual or the group would provide the more correct answer would also affect individual opinion. Asch would support earlier studies on this affect proving obvious links among social influence and individual opinion.

Asch's Theoretical Approach to Social Behavior. Asch's theoretical approach toward social behavior is individual opinion distorts dependent on different social factors among a majority group. His approach is similar to the early approaches toward better defining the effects of social influence upon individual opinion. Asch's method of research would demonstrate how an individual can easily receive influence in straying from the independent opinion toward the conformist opinion. According to Asch respondents, the reasons for their conformist attitudes would be feelings of wrongfulness, not wanting to ruin the study, the group was following along, and the group was experiencing an optical illusion. Asch would prove the strength of the unanimous majority, at which point group number can affect individual opinion, how partnership can strengthen personal opinion, and how abandonment of partnership effects individual opinion. Asch's approach is most successful in demonstrating the abandonment of independent opinion and acceptance of a majority opinion. The manipulation of variables among Asch's study further would support his theoretical approach to social behavior as independent opinion can receive manipulation from majority groups (Asch, 1955).

Research Methodology of Asch's Study. The study takes a group of seven to nine college students each male and assembles the group for a psychological experiment. The respondents are shown two white cards on one is a lone vertical black line and the other consists of three vertical lines varying in length. Respondents are asked to select the line matching the sole line on the other card. The lengths of the lines are substantially different. The experimenter told the other group members to give wrong responses in unanimity. The focal subject to the experiment is the individual unaware to this prearrangement. Of the 18 trials only six times would the group respond correctly. This study would occur among 123 individuals. The occurrence of error in such a situation is less than one-percent yet in this case the wrong judgments appear by the respondent 36.8-percent of the time (Asch, 1955, p. 3). A question arises of which is more influential the unanimity of a group or the size of a group. The opposition group would range from one to 15 people. When only one person would oppose the individual's instincts he would continue the process of independent response. A group of two opposers would result in the acceptance of the wrong response 13.6% of the time. When facing the pressures of a unanimous majority of three respondent error would increase to 31.8%. Substantial differences in respondent error would not occur upon increasing the size of the majority further. Breaking the unanimity of a group can have an effect on individual decision-making. This experiment would involve an individual who knowingly would or unknowingly give the truthful statement. With the presence of an individual breaking the unanimity of the group the individual respondent would answer incorrectly only 25% of the time (Asch, 1955, p. 5). Another distortion of the experiment would involve an individual who would respond different from the majority but would give a response different from both the majority and respondent. The majority group would pick either the line closest to the correct answer each time or furthest from the correct answer each time. This variation would have a considerable effect on the respondent's response rate. When the dissenter responded more accurately to the respondent's inclinations the respondent's error rate would decrease to 21.5%. When the majority answers more closely to the respondent the error rate drops to only 9%. Another variation to the experiment would involve a partner giving correct answers with the respondent against a unanimous majority. The respondent would remain completely independent 18 of 27 times. If the respondent's partner would give into the majority after six trials the respondent's error ratio would increase greatly to the level of a unanimous majority (Asch, 1955, p. 5).

Asch's Approach to the Self and Social Conformity. Solomon Asch confronts respondents with a research approach to the self and social conformity. When viewing the self from the point of view of William James it would seem Asch confronts the respondents' needs to possess recognition from others. It appears the social self crumbles as independence dissipates and social conformity prevails despite the human capacity to remain independent. Asch's experiments would show the individual to be no more than a creature of the world lacking the capacity of a creator.

Creators of his or her personal and social world benefit from experiences of freedom and from being able to view him or herself as agents rather than pawns of external forces . . . People are also creatures of his or her worlds. Biological factors, past experience, and the present situation powerfully shape behavior. (Bolt, 2004)

Asch eposes respondents in determining whether or not he or she maintains his or her human capacity to remain independent. When facing a unanimous majority of three or more people in opposition of an independent opinion a third of the group will retreat toward the comfort and safety of social conformity. This is perhaps an attempt at protecting a fragile social self ever convincing and altering from face to face. Asch provides statistics for his study less than one-percent respondent error should be present. His study involves two cards with a lone line on one card and three lines of obvious different sizes on the other card. The group of seven to nine possess the request to state, which of the three lines match the sole line on the other card. Twenty-seven trials would occur and 123 participants through variations of the same study take place (Asch, 1955, p. 3). Of this group of seven to nine only one participant receives a measure as the rest receive instructions when to respond incorrectly to measure the effects of social influence. Asch's approach is similar to the approaches taken by the earliest social psychology researchers during the beginning stages of the twentieth century. Asch would prove group opinion to be a persuasive force. Through the manipulation of experimental variables he would provide a better indication of just how compelling the power of social influence can be on independent opinion. To protect the social self the individual would often yield to social conformity. With the presence of a partner in challenging the social majority individual independence would increase. The abandonment of this partner to the social unanimous majority would cause individual independence to cease at the same rate were the partnership never to occur. Groups of one and two are less influential on individual independence than groups of three or more (Asch, 1955, p. 5). Asch would also prove content can better sway the individual toward social conformity.

Asch's approach is traditional in the sense of its past practice, and he does an excellent job of strengthening past test results and making conclusions on the occurrence of social conformity.

Conclusion. Group pressure does, in fact, influence individual opinion by as much as 36.8% in the case of a unanimous majority opinion of nine individuals (Asch, 1955, p. 3). When a unanimous majority of three individuals exists this number will not significantly vary. A group of two could change the opinion of a respondent 14% of the time. One other individual could not influence the opinion of a respondent. A partner to the respondent would increase independence from a unanimous majority lowering the error rate of the respondent from 37% to 25%. When the partner's response was more correct (selecting the line closest to the correct of the three) the respondent error rate would be 21.8%. When the group was more correct than the partner independence would vastly increase with a 9% rate of respondent error. Abandonment of a partner in the middle of a trial would increase error rate to the rate of a unanimous majority (Asch, 1955, p. 5). Asch's study would involve 123 separate trials.

Asch demonstrates the effect of social pressures on opinion. Even if an individual believes the group is wrong, he or she may conform in this case not to ruin the study, finding the group to be sheep, or general feelings of doubt (Asch, 1955, p. 4). Asch would find social factors to distort individual opinion. It would seem the need to receive recognition from others may contribute to the process of social conformity. Asch would finish his career as a pioneer of social and gestalt psychology.

Psychology in Action Part II

"Psychology in Action Part II" is in itself comprising of two parts. The first part involves a lone question matrix pertaining to the implications of Asch's study in terms of prejudice, discrimination, and diversity. The second segment of the paper involves an evaluation of the usefulness of the findings of Asch's study in terms of modern-day application. Asch's studies convincingly demonstrate without a doubt social conformity exists taking the place of independent thinking. The question can arise of whether or not social conformity can be a trait of leadership.

Implications of Asch's Study

Prejudice, Discrimination, and Diversity. In determining the implications of Asch's study in terms of prejudice, discrimination, and diversity it can be useful to define first the terms. Prejudice is an attitude toward another group where stereotypes are the formation of generalizations of this other group (Kenrick, Neuberg, & Cialdini, 2010, p. 362). Discrimination makes reference to behaviors directed toward an individual because of his or her group affiliation. Diversity in terms of race references interrelating groups of people living, working, and surviving together. Asch's study may demonstrate how prejudice, discrimination, and diversity is a product of social influence. If one is a member of a large group of individuals, and the group is a majority group of racists chances are an individual may conform to such attitudes despite personal beliefs. Such a prejudiced group would demonstrate discrimination and avoid instances of diversity. Asch's study would also demonstrate how prejudice and discrimination would become absent in a group of people who promote cultural diversity. In such a group an individual could remain independent of his or her mode of thinking. Conversely, a group promoting diversity can influence the racist individual to demonstrate behaviors acting against prejudice and racism. In both cases according to Asch's study prejudice, discrimination, and diversity may be no more than a social construction (Asch, 1955).

Utility of Asch's Study for Modern-day Application

Leadership, Social Responsibility, Individual Satisfaction. Asch's study would demonstrate the effects of a majority group on individual opinion. The dependent variable in the study would be the response of the respondent. The independent variable would be the dissenting group who could vary in size, involve partnership with the respondent, respond to greater or less correct responses than the respondent, or a partner could abandon the respondent. In each of these cases the response error rate of the respondent would fluctuate demonstrating without a doubt social opinion effects individual independence and rate of social conformity (Asch, 1955). It may be important to understand the utility of Asch's study for social psychology to possess any positive traits. After all what good is it to understand how group influence affects the individual if this knowledge is not put forth toward utility. The cigarette companies understood the effects of their social influence on the individual. The utility of Asch's study in this sense would possess grave negative effects in decreased life expectancy, increases in heart attack, and lung cancer. Surely Asch's work would bear some positive results regarding how the individual receives forceful persuasion into social conformity despite the preference toward independence. The fan who tips over the car after the baseball game surely would not do so without the social influence of his fellow comrades. Out of the negativity present within social influence may lie the ability to self-enhance. As others are influential in a group, they cannot convince an individual, he or she is better. Asch's studies proves, although these comparisons with others can modify personal opinion on a subject, the group continues to fail to convince the individual he or she is not superior. The individual continues to possess a more accurate depiction of the self, and Asch's studies can demonstrate how social influence does not necessarily make a negative impact on self-esteem (Hodges, 2004).

In applying Asch's studies to modern day one must consider the authority the unanimous and majority group may possess on individual opinion. Arming oneself with such knowledge one can make a positive influence on modern day circumstances. Society in itself one may view as a construction of a social opinion of the majority group. The majority group can often decide the greatest good for the greatest number of people. After all as the superior number the majority represents can achieve the greatest good through the self-seeking pursuit for happiness. In this pursuit individual opinion can modify in the direction of a social majority possessing positive influence when the goal is social utility. Arising new laws can be an example of social influence on individual opinion. People act upon the normative standards of a society many of which are a creation of the social majority. It may be the independent individual is in actuality acting in behalf of the social majority. Leadership can be at the root of the social majority creating a social group capable of influencing others with a positive message. These messages can involve laws catering to the autonomy of the individual. Whether leadership is transactional or transformational it may be a combination of transformational and transactional leadership creating the setting putting Asch's study into use on a much broader stage (Bass & Avolio, 1993). The charisma of the individual may make him or her better capable of leadership. It may not be charisma but instead reinforcement creating and driving a group in the direction of individual conformity. Asch does not speak so much of the reward of conformity, yet does describe feelings of doubt and "unequilibrium" acting as a form of punishment. Asch poses the question of perhaps leaders possess more independence (Asch, 1955, p. 5). Asch may recommend the individual who yearns for leadership to remain true to his or her opinions despite the presence of a social majority challenging individual independence. In understanding Asch's contribution to social psychology one may better be capable of affording social responsibility upon a network of individuals. The attitudes of the network can represent the attitudes of the majority within Asch's study. In conforming to the attitudes of the network one can increase individual satisfaction. Perhaps at other times a leader may need to conform to a group to attain the goal of social responsibility. In Asch's study no one is correct as conforming to the group almost becomes necessity. The necessity of conforming within Asch's study may be a positive influence in the workplace in understanding how social behavior cannot only be influential on behavior but also how one may cater to the social majority in creating a more socially responsible environment (DuBoff, 1989).

Conclusion. Asch's study is a true demonstration of social psychology the study of how environmental behaviors affect the individual. In Asch's study an individual will often let a group change his opinion even when he believes he is correct. Asch's approach to social behavior is the individual will, in fact, conform to social pressures. Asch in making use of the experimental method demonstrates how social settings affect one's ability to remain independent. Asch's study consists of modern day relevance in its effects on leadership, social responsibility, and individual satisfaction (Asch, 1955).

Psychology in Action Part III

"Psychology in Action Part III" involves an analysis of the significance to the Asch study in terms of understanding group formation, group dynamics, and intergroup relations. In addition an evaluation should occur of the influence of the major theoretical perspectives of social psychology on the interpretation of the significance of the Asch study. The significance to the Asch study is no secret demonstrating to what effect social pressures can influence individual opinion. The groups within the Asch study are a construction of his own planning in supporting earlier findings and creating findings uniquely his own. Social psychology focuses on the scientific study of social thinking, social influence, and social relations. The timing and nature of Asch's study would make his studies a potential hallmark of the field.

Significance of Asch's Study in Understanding Group Formation, Group Dynamics, and Intergroup Relations

Group formation. A group is a collection of people with as few as two people composing the group. In Asch's study the group one would not consider a "real group." A real group is a close relation such as a team or coworkers. The grouping that occurs in Asch's study although the individuals possess little common identity remain influential on members of the grouping. Groups can form in different means through non-groups, groupings, and real groups (Kenrick, Neuberg, & Cialdini, 2010, p. 410). An individual walking through the park may be part of a non-group possessing no structure in relation to other members, no influence, no common identity, or dependency on one another. These groups can form at any time walking through the park, driving on the freeway, or other means in which strangers become part of one's landscape. Non-groups can develop into groupings when these individuals become influential on one another. This can be as simple as waiting in a line with the stranger who walked by one in the park. Groupings possess the same characteristics of non-groups minus individuals can, in fact, influence one another. Asch demonstrates the influential abilities within groupings through his formation of a group. Asch tells eight of nine people to respond incorrectly after two trials of an 18 trial experiment. The lone individual the respondent becomes influenced by the unanimous majority as the error ratio increases from less than one-percent to nearly 37% (Asch, 1955, p. 3). As Asch modifies the experimental conditions the responses of the respondent become more predictable. Asch's group consists of all the characteristics of a grouping not depending on each other, sharing little common identity, no structural relations, yet are influential. The cohesion of the grouping seems to intimidate the respondent creating a situation in which the respondent's role is not clarified. In either case Asch's grouping demonstrates the force of majority and unanimous opinion on individual independence and the formation of social conformity to the group.

Group dynamics. The dynamics of a group makes reference to a behavioral system within a social group. The psychological processes within this behavioral system are part of the group dynamic. In Asch's study the result could be predictable to some extent as Asch would be remaking early twentieth century studies to solidify the findings. He would without a doubt demonstrate the experiments on social influence during the early twentieth century to be accurate. The dynamical system within Asch's study may be the creation of his altering the experiment as he would see fit. It is in this sense the Asch study would evolve over time from the studies during the early twentieth century (Kenrick, Neuberg, & Cialdini, 2010, p. 407). The dynamics of Asch's grouping is somewhat peculiar as some would say the involvement of deceit occurs. Eight of nine participants receive a request to respond incorrectly leaving a lone respondent to figure out what is happening. The individual would know each group member is unanimously wrong as the size of the lines to match are of obvious different sizes. Despite this the respondent would answer incorrectly 37% of the time. Asch measures the behavior of the respondent a result of the group behavior. Upon interviewing respondents after the experiment the independent respondents would state their confidence in their judgment would keep them from swaying toward an incorrect majority. This would be despite feelings of doubt and unequilibrium. Some would claim perceptions of the majority to be correct yet remain compelled to answer upon self-convictions. The group giving-in to social influence would state they believe they were simply wrong because of a unanimous majority. Others would claim he or she did not want to ruin the study. Others would find the majority group to be no more than sheep following one another along. This did not free them from following the unanimous wrong response (Asch, 1955, p. 4). This demonstrates the psychological processes of the respondent within the group dynamic. The system of behaviors within Asch's study although somewhat peculiar clearly demonstrate the effects of social influence on individual opinion.

Intergroup relations. Intergroup relations references interaction of one identifiable group with that of another or different identifiable group. Individual members interacting with different identifiable groups or the members thereof would too represent an intergroup relation. Prejudice, racism, and discrimination are examples of intergroup relations (Kenrick, Neuberg, & Cialdini, 2010, p. 410). Intergroups do not necessarily relate in such a negative manner. The relationship among groups is or can often be a result of the social influence of the members of a group as Asch's study would demonstrate (Asch, 1955). Members of a group advocating hate toward another group can influence others who may come across their group to demonstrate similar racist, prejudiced, and discriminatory behaviors. Conversely members of a group who promote diversity and positive relations with other groups, its members and new members become more likely to demonstrate positive behaviors. Asch's study shows even when an individual believes the group is wrong, more than a third of the time the individual will support wrongfully the group's opinion. Whether the opinion is of size of lines or racist implications the same effect is occurring pertaining to social influence and individual opinion. Group members are single units of the larger group whose individual opinions influence and dictate the occurrence and method of relating with other groups. Asch also demonstrates how attitudes can change and dissenters of group opinion can change how a group interrelates with other groups. The dynamic of a group is not a constant meaning neither is the means in which groups interrelate with other groups.

Influence of Major Theoretical Perspectives of Social Psychology on Interpretation of the Significance of Asch's Study

Sociocultural, evolutionary, social learning, and social cognitive perspectives. Within social psychology are four perspectives the sociocultural, evolutionary, social learning, and social cognitive perspective. The sociocultural perspective is the search for socially behavioral causes the influence of the larger group (Kenrick, Neuberg, & Cialdini, 2010, p. 7). The evolutionary perspective is the search for the socially behavioral causes as psychological and physical predispositions. The same predispositions permitting the reproduction and survival of ancestors (p. 8). The focus of the social learning perspective is on prior learning experience determining the social behaviors of the individual (p. 10). The focus of the social cognitive perspective is on the role of the mental processes in interpreting and memory retrieval of social experiences (p. 11).

Sociocultural and evolutionary perspectives. The significance of the Asch study is it demonstrates how individual opinion can be altered by social pressures and that individual opinion may be no more than a social construction. In Asch's study from a sociocultural perspective it is very easy to demonstrate how social behavior receives influence through a social group. The basis to this study from a sociocultural perspective does a superior job in demonstrating the effects of social opinion. Asch shows even when a unanimous group is obviously wrong in the eyes of the individual he or she will respond incorrectly 37% of the time (Asch, 1955, p. 3). The behavior of the individual changes as the social group changes their behavior. The group could change the individual's thought pattern and his responses as altered 37% of the time would demonstrate a change in behavior the result of social influence from a social group. From an evolutionary perspective perhaps reasons for conforming to group opinion are the same social behaviors allowing ancestors to survive and reproduce. From this perspective many would find not conforming to a unanimous and majority group to create an unsuitable environment to survive and reproduce. The psychological predisposition to conform may be a product of evolution (Kenrick, Neuberg, & Cialdini, 2010, p. 8).

Social learning and social cognitive perspectives. From a social learning perspective the respondents' decision to conform may be the result of prior experience. Perhaps the individual who conforms did not conform in a past situation and would receive reinforcement negatively for doing so. Conversely perhaps an individual who conforms would receive positive reinforcement in prior experiences, which would in turn influence present and future decisions to conform to social groups and the arising pressures of these groups (Kenrick, Neuberg, & Cialdini, 2010, p. 10). The social cognitive perspective would focus on the mental processes involved in the interpretation of Asch's experiment. This experience would become part of the individual's prior experience influencing future decisions from a social learning perspective. The experiment can either increase an individual's tendency to conform, decrease tendency, or possess no effect. If the individual took the study again would he or she be more likely to remain independent. One opinion may be the mental processes involved in such a social experience may increase individual independence decreasing social conformity concurrently (p.11).

Conclusion. The significance to the use of grouping in Asch's study demonstrates the force of majority and unanimous opinion on individual independence and the formation of social conformity to the group. The system of behaviors within Asch's study is significant in demonstrating the effects of social influence on individual opinion. Asch demonstrates how attitudes can change and dissenters of group opinion can change how a group interrelates with other groups (Asch, 1955, p. 5). The significance of the Asch study is it demonstrates how individual opinion can be altered by social pressures and that individual opinion may be no more than a social construction. From a sociocultural perspective it is the behaviors of the social group causing the individual to alter his opinion. The significance of the Asch study is it may demonstrate the psychological predisposition to conform may be a product of evolution. The social learning perspective takes the point of view the respondents' decision to conform may be the result of prior experiences. Finally, the social cognitive perspective focusing on the mental processes in the interpretation of the experimentation considers the effect Asch's study would possess on these 123 respondents within their future decision-making (Kenrick, Neuberg, & Cialdini, 2010, p. 7).

Influence of Major Theoretical Perspectives of Social Psychology on Interpretation of the Significance of Asch's Study

Sociocultural, evolutionary, social learning, and social cognitive perspectives. Within social psychology are four perspectives the sociocultural, evolutionary, social learning, and social cognitive perspective. The sociocultural perspective is the search for socially behavioral causes the influence of the larger group (Kenrick, Neuberg, & Cialdini, 2010, p. 7). The evolutionary perspective is the search for the socially behavioral causes as psychological and physical predispositions. The same predispositions permitting the reproduction and survival of ancestors (p. 8). The focus of the social learning perspective is on prior learning experience determining the social behaviors of the individual (p. 10). The focus of the social cognitive perspective is on the role of the mental processes in interpreting and memory retrieval of social experiences (p. 11).

Sociocultural and evolutionary perspectives. The significance of the Asch study is it demonstrates how individual opinion can be altered by social pressures and that individual opinion may be no more than a social construction. In Asch's study from a sociocultural perspective it is very easy to demonstrate how social behavior receives influence through a social group. The basis to this study from a sociocultural perspective does a superior job in demonstrating the effects of social opinion. Asch shows even when a unanimous group is obviously wrong in the eyes of the individual he or she will respond incorrectly 37% of the time (Asch, 1955, p. 3). The behavior of the individual changes as the social group changes their behavior. The group could change the individual's thought pattern and his responses as altered 37% of the time would demonstrate a change in behavior the result of social influence from a social group. From an evolutionary perspective perhaps reasons for conforming to group opinion are the same social behaviors allowing ancestors to survive and reproduce. From this perspective many would find not conforming to a unanimous and majority group to create an unsuitable environment to survive and reproduce. The psychological predisposition to conform may be a product of evolution (Kenrick, Neuberg, & Cialdini, 2010, p. 8).

Social learning and social cognitive perspectives. From a social learning perspective the respondents' decision to conform may be the result of prior experience. Perhaps the individual who conforms did not conform in a past situation and would receive reinforcement negatively for doing so. Conversely perhaps an individual who conforms would receive positive reinforcement in prior experiences, which would in turn influence present and future decisions to conform to social groups and the arising pressures of these groups (Kenrick, Neuberg, & Cialdini, 2010, p. 10). The social cognitive perspective would focus on the mental processes involved in the interpretation of Asch's experiment. This experience would become part of the individual's prior experience influencing future decisions from a social learning perspective. The experiment can either increase an individual's tendency to conform, decrease tendency, or possess no effect. If the individual took the study again would he or she be more likely to remain independent. One opinion may be the mental processes involved in such a social experience may increase individual independence decreasing social conformity concurrently (p.11).

Conclusion. The significance to the use of grouping in Asch's study demonstrates the force of majority and unanimous opinion on individual independence and the formation of social conformity to the group. The system of behaviors within Asch's study is significant in demonstrating the effects of social influence on individual opinion. Asch demonstrates how attitudes can change and dissenters of group opinion can change how a group interrelates with other groups (Asch, 1955, p. 5). The significance of the Asch study is it demonstrates how individual opinion can be altered by social pressures and that individual opinion may be no more than a social construction. From a sociocultural perspective it is the behaviors of the social group causing the individual to alter his opinion. The significance of the Asch study is it may demonstrate the psychological predisposition to conform may be a product of evolution. The social learning perspective takes the point of view the respondents' decision to conform may be the result of prior experiences. Finally, the social cognitive perspective focusing on the mental processes in the interpretation of the experimentation considers the effect Asch's study would possess on these 123 respondents within their future decision-making (Kenrick, Neuberg, & Cialdini, 2010, p. 7).

Carley, S. G. (2013). *Independence versus conformity, revisiting a Solomon E Asch study: Psychology in action*. Boston: SGC.

Psychology in Action Part IV

Psychology in Action Matrix

Implications of the study's findings on how researchers and practitioners interpret personality and personality related behaviors. The findings of the study would imply researchers or in this case Solomon E Asch to interpret personality as a product of social influence. Asch may view independence to occur a majority of the time. In the face of a unanimous majority conformity occurs over one-third of the time (Asch, 1955, p. 3). With such an increase in the margin of error when facing a unanimous majority, Asch would find independence not to be a consistent trait, and one that easily fluctuates basing upon the social environment. Asch may consider the social self of the individual adapting to situations to fit the many roles in his or her life (Lawson, Graham, & Baker, 2007). In which roles does a person remain independent and in which roles does, he or she conform. Asch may view the personality of each individual a product of conforming to his or her various social environments as evidenced by the results of his study on social pressures and opinions.

Study evaluation and validity. The validity of a test is dependent on its ability to measure accurately the unit in which the test designs (Kenrick, Neuberg, & Cialdini, 2010, p. 22). The findings of the study are convincing in regard to demonstrating how groups can change individual opinion. In the case of the Asch study this occurs despite the majority/unanimous group as obviously wrong. Asch's modifications of the study demonstrate a group's wrong opinion, as closer to one's opinion can possess an even greater effect on socially influencing others. Dissenters of a group can diminish social conformity and traitors to a social group can increase individual conformity to its greatest levels (Asch, 1955, p. 5). The study is a good means of proving how social groups effect individual independence. The condition in which the findings are valid does occur. The study sets out to measure the rate of individual conformity to a social group, which it has done. The study is truly a valid measure of opinion and social pressure. If the study were to set out to demonstrate how positive reinforcement effects greyhounds or some unrelated study, the condition of Asch's study could be found an invalid measure. As it stands Asch does an excellent job of validating his study using social psychology perspectives.

Relation of Santee & Maslach and Milgram study to Asch study and social psychology. Stanley Milgram's experiment may be an example of how social pressures can influence individual opinion. This study is less ethical than Asch's study despite the fact no individuals are experiencing any pain, minus the respondent who experiences a brief test shock of 45 volts. The individual is led to believe he or she will be in trouble if he or she do not finish the experiment. In the process assuring the individual the shocks possess no long-term effects. This is during the subject who is not receiving shocks in reality, is screaming for the shocks to stop at 150 volts. Despite this 65% of the respondents continue to an amazing 450 volts. The predictor was for one percent to continue to the end. Only four percent expect to continue past a danger zone where the individual is unresponsive. This compares to a 75% rate of individuals continuing the shock past an unresponsive to desperately screaming for help person (Kenrick, Neuberg, & Cialdini, 2010, p. 189). One can assume these people would not deliver any shocks without social influence. In this case it is individual leadership and authority as opposed to majority influence. In both cases social pressure alters individual opinion.

Santee and Maslach study opinions focusing not on the conformists as Asch but instead conversely focuses on non-conformists. Participants would be asked their opinion on a situation after hearing the opinions of three other people. This is the amount, according to Asch at which individuals become more inclined to conform. Another group, the control group would not listen to the opinions of others before extending his or her opinion. The experiment would start with participants taking the Texas Social Behavior Inventory. One to three weeks later groups of four participants would be assigned to either a control group or a peer-opinion conditioned group. The peer-opinion group would listen to the responses of the other members of the group before responding to the 20 questions. Conformity would measure through frequency of "good" responses as judged by undergraduate judges. This would be the majority choice of four choices, including a minority choice, poor choice, and to write in one's own choice. The results were the peer opinion condition would increase conformity by 12%. In addition when the peer-opinion group was unanimous the response rate for the majority choice would increase by an additional 7% (Santee & Maslach, 1982). Santee and Maslach would make the same conclusion as Asch in social conformity increases when presented with the opinions of a group. Santee and Maslach's study just as Asch demonstrates the effects of social influence on individual opinion. For this reason these studies would classify within the subdiscipline of social psychology.

Description of how Santee & Maslach and Milgram support Asch study. Milgram's study is one in which would support Asch's findings. Milgram's study examines social pressure less from the viewpoint of groups applying the pressure but instead an authority figure. This authority figure is part of a group as he hides behind a group in stating the participant will be in trouble if he or she does not finish. In this sense it is the same group pressures influencing and changing individual opinions. An individual shocking another against his or her will would have to be next to impossible. It would have to be only the forces of social pressures causing one to engage in such activity. The 65% who continue the shockings until stopped by the experimenter definitively demonstrate the effects of social pressure on opinion. In the process Milgram's studies would further support the studies by Solomon Asch on social pressures and opinion. Asch supports the influence of social pressures on opinion through the use of two cards, one with a lone line and the other with three lines of obvious different size. A group is told to give the wrong response after two trials, and one respondent is left for the remainder of the 16 trials to figure out why the group is giving the wrong response every time. In any case the individual conforms 36.8% to a unanimous group of eight demonstrating the effects of social influence on opinion (Asch, 1955, p. 3). Milgram supports Asch's claim by making a participant believe he or she is shocking an individual for responding incorrectly. He starts with a small shock to the person of 45 watts. Milgram threatens the person shocking another not to stop, and 65% of participants receive social influence to shock a person up to 450 volts until the experimenter stops him or her. The person shocking does not know the shocks are not administering. Despite desperate pleas an individual will continue to administer lethal shocks to another under the influence of social pressure. Santee and Maslach would also support Asch's claim social pressures influence individual opinions. As respondents' answers become more the same when aware of the individual and group opinions of other respondents, Asch's claim gains increased validity and reliability for that matter, as time and again individuals are becoming influenced by a group.

Asch, Milgram, and Santee & Maslach

The following report involves a discussion of the various methodologies and instrumentations across three studies in terms of future studies. The creation of a chart will occur comparing the methodologies and instrumentations used within the original study versus the two selected follow-up studies. The original study, of course, is the 1955 Asch study on social pressures and opinions. The two follow-up studies include Stanley Milgram's 1963 study on obedience and a Santee and Maslach study on opinion. The two follow-up studies would be in the attempt of supporting Asch in his findings social pressures, in fact, do possess a definitive effect on individual opinion.

Effect of various methodologies and instrumentations across the three studies in terms of future studies. Future studies from a social learning perspective may use the Asch, Milgram, and Santee and Maslach studies to create even more elaborate means of demonstrating the effects of social pressures on individual opinion. Asch's method and instrumentation would begin with the selection of a panel of seven to nine male college students. The experiment makes use of visual judgment comparing the length of lines. Two white cards are shown to the respondents with a vertical black line on one and three vertical black lines of obvious different sizes on the other. Respondents by request select the line on the card of three, which matches the sole line on the other card keeping in mind the lengths of the three vertical lines are substantially different. During the third of the 18 trials eight of the respondents unanimously answer incorrectly leaving a lone respondent to ponder the situation. The experimenter has told eight of the participants to answer incorrectly after the first two rounds. They answer correctly only six of the 18 times. Asch is measuring the effects this will possess on the lone respondent. Asch runs this experiment 123 times finding 36.8% of the time respondents will answer incorrectly to yield to the unanimous majority group. The rate of error is normally less than one percent comparing to the 36.8% rate within the experiment. A unanimous majority of two opposers would lower the error ratio to 13.6%. When the unanimous majority would consist of three members the error rate would not significantly change from 15 members remaining at 31.8%. A single opposer would possess no affect. Two dissenters from a unanimous majority decreases the error ratio to 25%. When the respondent's partner or second dissenter would answer more accurately than the unanimous group the error ratio would be 21.5%. This is to say selecting the line closer to the correct one, comparing to the group selecting the line obviously incorrect from the sole line on the other card. When the group selects the more correct option than the second dissenter, the error ratio drops to 9%. A partner to a respondent giving correct answers who abandons the individual for the unanimous majority after six trials, the respondent error rate will return to the level of the unanimous majority 36.8% (Asch, 1955, p. 5).

Santee and Maslach study. Within the Santee and Maslach study participants would be asked their opinion on a situation dividing participants into two groups. The experiment begins with study participants taking the Texas Social Behavior Inventory. Upon completion of the inventory one to three weeks from this time, groups of four participants would meet assignment to either the control group or the peer-opinion conditioned group. The difference among the two groups is the peer-opinion conditioned group listens to the opinions of the three group members before responding. The measure of conformity would occur through frequency of "good" responses according to undergraduate judges. A good response as the majority choice would conflict the other three choices, including a minority choice, poor choice, and creative dissent. The results are conformity would increase by 12% within the peer opinion condition. In addition the response rate for the majority choice would increase by an additional 7% when the peer-opinion group was unanimous (Santee & Maslach, 1982).

Stanley Milgram Experiment. It would occur not so long ago during the 1960s Stanley Milgram (1963) would conduct his studies at Yale University. The design would involve a devient experimenter telling his participants they are part of an examination on the effect of negative reinforcement on the process of learning. These studies can support Asch's claim social pressures distort individual opinion. Participants receive instruction to punish the learner in the next room who is a research assistant. This should occur whenever the learner makes an error using an instrument, he or she are under the belief to be a shock generator. The switches among the panel label from 15 to 450 volts representing a severe shock. Keep in mind a maximum electroconvulsive shock within electroconvulsive therapy is 140 volts for a period of less than one-half second (Corner, 2005). The participant first receives a jolt with a 45 volt shock to understand the discomfort the other person would experience. Participants receive instruction from the experimenter to begin through the administration of a slight shock, and each time the learner makes an error the voltage increases. The learner is not receiving shocks, yet participants possess no reason to believe otherwise, especially basing upon the protests from the other room, which would turn to screaming and pounding on the wall as the punishment should increase. Prior to the conduction of the study, Milgram would ask social scientists of their estimation of the number of participants going to the extreme 450 volts. The estimation of the experts is a group of one percent could perhaps demonstrate this level of deviation (Kenrick, Neuberg, & Cialdini, 2010, p. 189). The experts' estimation is vastly wrong. Sixty-five percent of the participants would administer the full 450 volts. This is despite an unresponsive learner apparently either dead or unconscious. A total of 75% continue to administer shocks even when the person is apparently dead or unconscious. Many participants clearly sense distress from the experience, but continue to look to the requester for permission to continue of which he condones and promotes their behaviors. When the participants inquire of their liability for any injuries the learner should experience, the experimenter insists the responsibility is his, and the procedure should continue.

Conclusion. Future studies can create even more elaborate means of demonstrating the effects of social pressures on individual opinion through the use of Asch, Milgram, and Santee and Maslach experimentation and instrumentation. Milgram and Santee and Maslach would support Asch's findings of the effects of social pressures on individual opinion. Santee and Maslach in their study would find conformity would increase by 12% within the peer opinion condition supporting Asch. Milgram would find through his form of social influence he could make 65% of participants risk physical harm. Milgram's study would support Asch more than any it would seem. It may be the fragility of the social self, resulting in such extreme conformity and obedience (Lawson, Graham, & Baker, 2007).

Chart Comparing Methodology and Instrumentation of Asch Study to Milgram and Santee and Maslach Study

Unanimous majority, unanimous majority of three, unanimous majority of two, two dissenters.

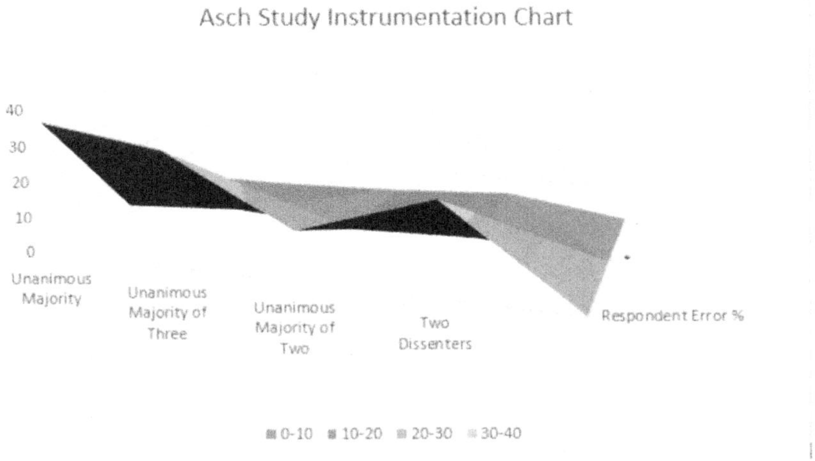

Carley, S. G. (2013). *Independence versus conformity, revisiting a Solomon E Asch study: Psychology in action*. Boston: SGC.

Chart Comparing Methodology and Instrumentation of Asch Study to Milgram and Santee and Maslach Study

More accurate dissenter, more accurate majority group, abandoning partner.

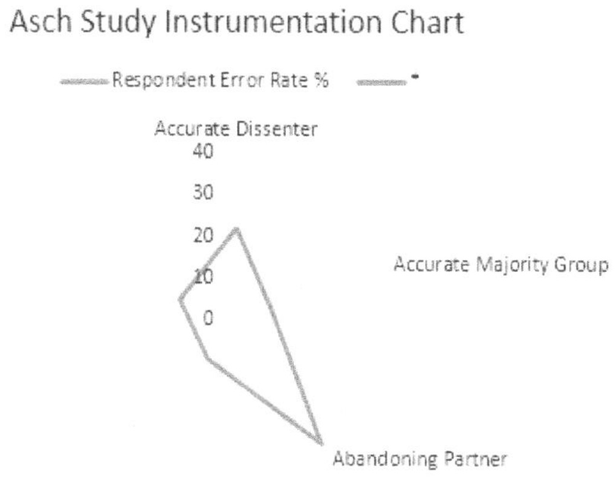

Chart Comparing Methodology and Instrumentation of Asch Study to Milgram and Santee and Maslach Study

Santee & Maslach instrumentation chart.

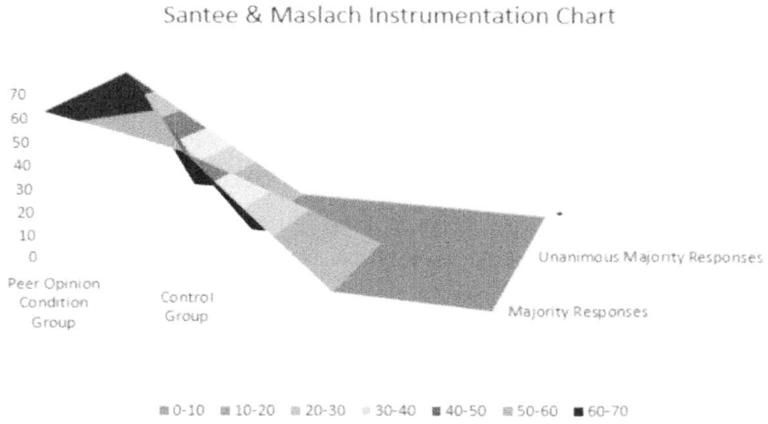

Carley, S. G. (2013). *Independence versus conformity, revisiting a Solomon E Asch study: Psychology in action*. Boston: SGC.

Chart Comparing Methodology and Instrumentation of Asch Study to Milgram and Santee and Maslach Study

Milgram instrumentation chart.

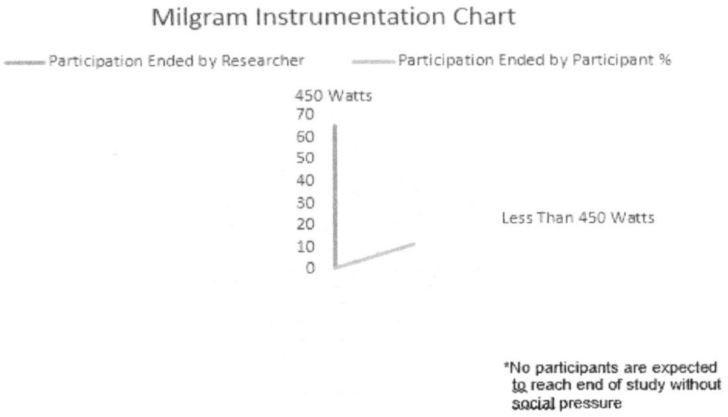

Psychology In Action Part V

Psychology in Action Matrix

Role social cognition played in the Asch study. Social cognition is a process of making sense of oneself and others. This involves the interpretation of others and any occurring mental processes. Social cognition consists of four core processes: memory, judgment, interpretation, and attention. Attention is a process of focusing on oneself or the immediate environment. In Asch's study it is the environment's effect on the respondent in which Asch would take measure. The respondent's attention to his environment would create an interpretation of a possible disturbance from expectations. The respondent's group, answering wrongly in a unanimous fashion would result in respondent conformity to the unanimous group opinion. To the respondent, the environment creates a situation in which, it would make sense to respond erroneously. The respondents may interpret the situation differently, some believing they are sheep following along, others finding themselves wrong, and others viewing the group as falling victim to an illusion. In each interpretation of the situation a demonstration of social cognition creates a scenario where the respondent can either remain independent or conform to social opinion (Kenrick, Neuberg, & Cialdini, p. 75). It is this social opinion making individual judgment difficult. Without the social opinion of the group, the individual would answer 99 – 100% how one should expect. With the presence of a unanimous majority answering incorrectly, the respondent's judgment fluctuates resulting in highly unpredictable responses. The unpredictability of the responses is visible with an error response rate increasing from less than one-percent to over 36% (Asch, 1955, p. 3). The experiment incorporates use of memory by answering as a group correctly once in a while so the respondent does not become suspicious. Asch's experiment does not involve memory so much as the other three factors of social cognition. The respondent after taking the experiment one may assume, his memory of the events would increase individual independence and reduce error response rates. At the same time it could be an individual may continue to follow the responses of the incorrect group to avoid any feelings of isolation. Most likely memory should reduce error rate (Kenrick, Neuberg, & Cialdini, p. 76).

Impact of the Asch study on social psychology. Social psychology is the scientific study of how people think about, influence, and relate to one another. Asch's study acts as fuel to social psychology as a demonstration of the effects of groups on the individual. Asch's study would make the science of social psychology more a scientific discipline and less a casual observation. Asch's study would support the earliest experiments of social psychology demonstrating how its founders and forefathers would lead its followers into a correct path. During the birth of social psychology, Bernheim's work would pertain to the effects of social groups and formation of crowds. Asch's studies would support these findings and verify the earliest works within social psychology to be accurate. If Asch did not support the findings of the earliest work within social psychology through 123 trials of his demonstration, it may be the very foundation of social psychology to base upon errors and lazy research. As it turns Asch would, in fact, support the earliest studies in social psychology demonstrating the opinions of a social group can cause individual opinion to change, and these changes are a direct result of the presence and opinions of the group (Asch, 1955). Implications of the Asch study for industrial organizational psychology. Industrial/organizational (IO) psychology is the science of the human aspect of organizations. This science involves research of company employees, and the application of the research statistics (Spector, 2008). Asch's study may infer pertaining to IO psychology, individual independence may be more useful within the working group environment. As is present within the Asch study, groups are wrongfully influencing individuals to make wrongful decisions to accommodate the unanimity of the group. In the workplace should the individual conform to the workgroup despite inclinations to do otherwise, this could be at the cost of production. It may be a difficult situation when facing a unanimous workgroup stating task performance should occur in a certain manner. The individual may possess feelings of doubt when confronted with such a situation. The easiest decision may be simply to conform to social opinion. The independent individual with feelings of doubt regarding a group's decision may be best to discuss his or her feelings for disagreeing with a work group. It may be their opinion is valuable and can improve the proficiency of the working group. One may also be capable of discussing the situation with a manager or supervisor to receive his or her feedback on the situation. The implications of Asch's study toward IO psychology certainly would require the individual to air his or her opinions. If not in front of the group in an open forum, perhaps in a private forum with a manager or supervisor to attain the best proficiency among the place of employment (Asch, 1955).

Psychology in Action Part V Section II

The second part of Psychology in Action Part V involves a proposal for a follow-up to the Solomon E Asch study on the effects of social pressures on individual opinions. The research question of the proposal is "How does Asch's research methodology improve the reliability and validity of his experiment?" The thesis to the research question is through repetitive trials and variations of his experiment Solomon E Asch would demonstrate both validity and reliability within his experiments. The theoretical framework supporting the hypothesis will make use of Asch's studies and statistics in demonstrating the reliability and validity of his study. The informative nature of Asch's article on Social Pressures and Opinion would permit the research to coincide exclusively with this one article. The goal is to succeed in demonstrating and finding the link among Asch's study demonstrating an increase in test reliability and test validity.

Outline of follow-up study objectives. The objectives within the follow-up of Asch's study involve providing the necessary input in supporting the statement Asch's repeated trials and variations to his study would increase both test validity and test reliability. In supporting the thesis a description of the research methodology should occur. A description should also occur of the theoretical framework supporting the hypothesis. The research methodology is present within the article Social Pressures and Opinions documenting the information within Asch's study. The theoretical framework will make use of the research methodology in demonstrating test validity and test reliability.

Description of proposed research methodology. With this qualitative study the research requires no more than the reading of Solomon E. Asch's (1955) Opinions and Social Pressure. Within this study the means of proceeding involves answering the research question of "How does Asch's research methodology improve the reliability and validity of his experiment?" In answering such a question the formation of a thesis should occur. The thesis to the research question is through repetitive trials and variations of his experiment, Asch would demonstrate both validity and reliability within his experiments. The activity of the research involves Asch's measurements of 123 trials of groupings of one to 15 members arranged around a lone respondent who Asch would measure (Asch, 1955, p. 3). The basic arrangement to Asch's experiment would involve seven to nine male college students requested to take part in a psychology experiment. The group are matching lines, on one card are three black lines on a white card of noticeably different sizes. On the second card is a lone line of which the group must match to the three lines on the other card. The group minus one individual upon request after two rounds starts giving the wrong responses for two-thirds of the 18 card selections. The error rate of the study is normally less than one-percent. The 36.8% respondent error rate when facing a unanimous majority would demonstrate, in fact, social pressures to influence opinion, and the demonstration would be a success. Asch's variations to the study would yield further information to the effects of social pressures on individual opinion as a unanimous group of three would be as influential as a unanimous group of 15. A unanimous group of two would decrease respondent error rate to 13.6%, and one individual giving wrong responses would possess of no affect. A partner to the respondent would result in an error rate of 21.5%. When the group was more correct than the second dissenter the respondent's error rate would drop to 9%. When a partner to the respondent would abandon him for the group, the respondent error rate would increase to that of the unanimous majority (p. 5). Asch's experiment is a success but what does this mean in terms of validity and reliability.

Theoretical framework supporting hypothesis. In answering the research question one should first understand the concepts of reliability and validity. Reliability makes reference to the consistency of the results of the tests. Validity makes reference to the tests ability to measure accurately that which the design intends (Kenrick, Neuberg, & Cialdini, 2010, p. 22). Asch's measurements of the respondent error rate can provide clues in responding to the research question in forming a thesis. In existence seems to be a relationship among test reliability and number of trials of the test, and a second relationship among test validity and the variations within Asch's study. In Asch's study he would perform the test 123 times (Asch, 1955, p. 3). In running the test so many times, one could recall the results of each test and determine if, in fact, the test results are accurate across the duration of trials. Asch's study would provide mean results pertaining to varying methodologies of conducting the study as one can recall through unanimous majority, varying sizes of unanimous majority, partnership, strength of error within partnership, and desertion of partnership (Asch, 1955, pp. 3 - 5). It would seem these variations of Asch's study would better demonstrate the validity of the test study. Asch's study is trying to measure accurately the effect of social pressures on individual opinions. Asch provides information on the rate of respondent error as less than one percent. As the respondent error increases and varies basing upon Asch's manipulation of the study variables the validity of the study becomes more prominent.

Conclusion. Solomon E Asch's study is originally a response to the earliest studies in social psychology pertaining to the effects of social influence on individual opinion. Psychology in Action Part V would go beyond personal opinion of the effects of the study. In responding to the question of, "How does Asch's research methodology improve the reliability and validity of his experiment?" it would be imperative to link Asch's methodology to a direct correlation of increases in test reliability and test validity. Asch's ability to measure accurately what the test design intends can relate to his ability to run variations of the study in altering the level of respondent error. Asch's use of 123 trials of the experiment would assist in increasing the reliability of the test. These two factors alone are the measure of success in responding to the research question. Through repeated trials and variations of his experiment Asch would demonstrate both validity and reliability within his experiments (Asch, 1955).

Psychology in Action Part VI

"Psychology in Action Part VI" involves the identification of an unused personality assessment instrument that may have been of use within the Solomon Asch study. In addition a description of the information that would receive gathering from the unidentified unused assessment instrument, and the potential benefit to the Asch study will occur. Finally a justification should occur pertinent to the selection and use of the identified instrument for use within the Asch Study. Asch would create an effective interview style experiment among a group of young men. This is not to say his experiment could not have taken place through the use of other reliable means of personality assessment instrument. This report is a somewhat hypothetical compilation of the Asch study making use of a different instrument of assessment.

Direct Self-report

Bernheim Style. The Asch study would take place interview style as he would sit face-to-face with the participant and other group members and take part in the demonstration. It is perhaps Asch did not need to take such involvement in the demonstration although his methods would be found most effective. A direct self-report could have been as equally effective as Asch's use of the face-to-face interview. Asch may have made the decision to create a multiple choice inventory for the respondent to fill-out (Cloninger, 2008, p. 14). After the respondent's answers meet submission, Asch could have made use of the option to create a more Bernheim style test. This would be one of the early tests within social psychology of which Asch would attempt to either support or disprove. It would be Bernheim as much of the motivation and inspiration for Asch to conduct his variation of a Bernheim study (Asch, 1955).

Direct Self-report Measures and Potential Benefits

Comparison of Dual Inventory. The unused assessment would gather first the data from the respondent's initial set of answers. After the passage of moderate time, the respondent could return to responding a second time to the same questions. Only this time the respondent would become aware of the opinions of peers and the governing authority. The direct self-report as a multiple choice inventory could gather the new responses of the respondent after learning of this new information. Some of this information may even be fictitious in better demonstrating how social opinion can affect independence and individual opinion. Upon completion of the second inventory, the two tests can meet comparison against one another, and the effects of social influence can measure. This may be a potential benefit to the study if Asch did not want to be as much of a part of the direct experimentation. Asch also would have the option of running this type of study in conjunction with his interview style experiment. Such a method would only create more support for the earliest social psychology studies.

Justification of Direct Self-report

Use Within the School System and Workplace. Direct self-report inventories are a popular means of assessing abilities and talents among many subjects. The school system often makes use of such a testing method in determining the intelligence of their student population. The workplace also makes use of this testing system as a pre-employment measure of ability. These direct self-report inventories also can be a means of determining advancement within a company. The wide use of the direct self-report inventory would seem to justify the use of this assessment instrument as an alternative within the Asch study. In addition, the original study would take place in a similar means, and although Asch may seem to have outdone Bernheim, the direct self-report inventory continues to be a reliable and satisfactory means of testing because of both its reliability and validity.

Conclusion. One such personality assessment instrument not used within the Asch study but have been would be the direct self-report. A multiple choice inventory with timely re-tests could have provided just as sufficient information involving the effect of social opinion on conformity (Cloninger, 2008, p. 14). The direct self-report would gather information from the participants through responses. A re-test of the participants at a later date would occur after suggesting to the participants, authorities and their peers would answer otherwise. A comparison of the two tests would yield a verifiable response to the question of social opinion's effect on independence. The use of the direct self-report in the school system and workplace as a testing and pre-employment measure would seem to justify the use of the direct self-report as an accurate assessment tool.

Psychology in Action Part VII

The Psychology in Action Part V meets a literature review within Psychology in Action Part VII. Part VII presents the author in a scenario as the individual following-up with the participants of the Asch study after their participation. The design of a 10-question survey, the creation of which would attempt to reveal information of the effects and expectations of the study on participants. One may expect in an experiment involving more than 1,000 individuals, the expectations of the study results may vary as well as the long-term effects. The questions within this study may not reveal the answers as one cannot go back in time and operate the follow-up study. Perhaps in resurrecting the study of Solomon Asch, a similar follow-up can reveal an accurate effect to that of the original participants.

"Psychology in Action Part VII" is a literature review of the Psychology in Action Part V in which a follow-up to the Solomon E Asch study would occur. Within this literature review will be a reflection on the literature and general knowledge pertaining to psychology. The creation of a survey driven personality assessment suitable for online completion should occur through a 10-question survey supporting the follow-up of the Asch study in this case. Finally a justification should involve the wording and inclusion of survey questions within the survey driven personality assessment. Part VII would incorporate more inclusion of the author in the experimentation than the original part V report.

Literature Review Supporting Follow-up to Asch Study

Long-term Effects of Study on Participants. The follow-up of the Psychology in Action Part V would consist originally of an in-depth review of Asch's methodologies and its effects on the reliability and validity of the experiment. In the Psychology in Action Part VII an assumption will occur of contact with the participants within the Asch experiment. During the study the focus of the experiment would be on a lone individual within the group, yet seeking any long-term effects among each and any member of the experiment may be as useful as the responses from the lone respondent. Participants may be best to meet privately separate from the means at which the experiment would take place. One may start by letting each participant aware of the results of the experiment asking their opinions of the results, and if before the study should occur if these were the results they would expect. The results as a major increase in the respondent error rate the result of majority opinion, even when this opinion is obviously incorrect. One may recall even a majority of 15 could not significantly alter individual opinion in comparison to groups of as small as three (Asch, 1955, p. 5). Comparing to groups of two who would be possess significant affect from the lack of numbers in providing an incorrect response. Still other factors would meet research, such as the effect of only a lone dissenter of a group of one, a teammate to the respondent providing correct responses. Still other times this second dissenter would provide even more incorrect responses than the group and at times less incorrect responses to the group. The effects of the teammate abandoning the respondent would meet measurement, all of which the group members must share some opinion of their expectations of the results (Asch, 1955, p. 5). This is the importance in inviting each participant to return for such a follow-up and not just the respondent. The long-term effects of the experiment may possess a similar effect on group members as it does on the respondent. Group members would only know of the deceit just prior to the experiment, whereas the respondent would not learn of the deceit until after the experiment. Questions may arise of the effects this experiment would possess on the group members in terms of their susceptibility to conforming or remaining independent. Different theories may arise of the effects this experiment could possess on group members, some stating conformity to increase and others who may state independence to decrease.

Following-up respondents may be best to study the result of each scenario with the group member. As an example, state the results of the unanimous group's effect over the course of the study and obtain an opinion from the group member if this meets their expectations. Next go to the results of the respondent possessing a teammate, and ask if the results would meet their expectations. No better means of assessing long-term effects of the study than asking the group members themselves. Without talking to the group members, one may only make an assumption on the effects of the experiment on the group members. Perhaps the effects would differ greatly from a respondent from a member of the experimental group in on the deceit with Solomon Asch. The assumption is such a study would possess the effect of an increase in independence and decrease in conformity. After taking part in such an experiment participants one may expect to increase independence. The result of the test will most likely possess the effect of causing a reaction in which an individual will more trust his or her instincts even within the presence of enhanced social pressures. The design of the study however may demonstrate the same tendency even in future circumstances for an individual to conform to adapt better to such situations (Asch, 1955).

Literature Reflection and Psychology Knowledge

Positive, Negative, or Neutral Effects of Study. Reflecting back upon the Asch experiment, it truly would increase personal knowledge base pertaining to psychology. The demonstration of behaviors within the Asch experiment would be peculiar, when in consideration, it would seem the entire experiment to be somewhat peculiar. The ethics to the study may come into question in consideration of the long-term effects the respondents and other group members may attain from their participation within the study. It would seem the expectancy of major change among the degree of social conformity among these participants. Perhaps a further study could occur to in some manner determine if the effects of the experiment are positive, negative, or if, in fact, bear any effect. The initial response of a 36.8% respondent error rate would be significant enough to make the claim social opinion affects individual decision-making. This in comparison to the less than 1% error rate of responders (Asch, 1955, p. 3). Asch would do a good job of distinguishing what is causing the conformity. It would be a majority group of three or more individuals responding incorrectly. Groups of less than three would not hold this effect, nor would a group possess this effect when the responder would have a partner. This study is a true demonstration of social psychology, the scientific study of how people think about, influence, and relate to one another (Myers, 2010). The entire basis of the Asch study focuses on the effects of social influence on the individual. The basis to the 1955 study would be a means of settling any past inaccuracies of studies on social influence. Asch would prove the respondents of the earliest studies to provide accurate studies and the research, in fact would not falsify. Despite assumptions opinions cannot easily distort, Asch would demonstrate otherwise. Asch would also have to prove the responses were not expectations of a respondent or the guidance of an experimenter in which case the distortion of opinions would not be an example of social influence. The assumption may be opinions cannot so easily distort. Perhaps as good subjects the respondents were simply giving the answers he or she expect to give. Perhaps a changing opinion was not social influence, but instead the guiding by an experimenter to create assumptions within the respondent. These assumptions and not social influence could distort opinion. Social influence is not devoid of critical thought and the ability to rise above social influence is part of human nature. It may be to change judgment, one first must change one's knowledge of a subject. Asch would seem to prove the variance in respondent responses not to be the inaccuracies of these assumptions, yet instead the presence of real life social influence.

10-Question Survey Supporting Follow-up Study

1. Could you offer any suggestions from a participant's point of view of a means to improve the testing experience?

2. Do you believe the 123 trials of the test to increase test reliability and validity?

3. Are you more likely to conform to a group when a partner shares your opinion?

4. Are you more likely to conform to majority groups of more than three compared to groups of one or two?

5. Are your responses to the previous two questions a result of the experiment? How has the experiment changed your response?

6. Do you think differently pertaining to social conformity as opposed to before taking part in the experiment?

7. Can you explain your interpretation of the results of the test?

8. Do you find the test to possess any negative long-term effects on your decision-making?

9. Were the results of the study what you would expect?

10. Do you believe the experiment to alter your degree of social conformity? If so, how?

Carley, S. G. (2013). *Independence versus conformity, revisiting a Solomon E Asch study: Psychology in action*. Boston: SGC.

Justification of Survey Questions

Individual Justification of Survey Questions. To justify the inclusion of the survey, it seems best to review each question individually. The first question would be a simple means of perhaps improving the experiment, which would turn to be a success. The second question to test the basic knowledge of the test member, and obtain their opinion on if the test would seem to score consistently and measure social opinion. The third question would be a sturdy follow-up and review of the test member's knowledge of the results. Question four similar to question three is a review of test member knowledge. Question five is a means of determining if the experiment is altering the test member's degree of influence from social opinion. It will also determine if and how the response would alter. Question six similarly is a determination of the long-term effects the study will possess on its participants. Question seven is a means of determining how a participant would construe the findings if, in fact, he would find social influence to be the major factor for the respondent's increase in erroneous responses. Question eight will assist in determining if any negative effects exist from the participation in the experiment, and if so what the effects are. The interest of question nine is in the expectations of the participant before taking part in the experiment, and if the results would match a participant's expectations. The final question speaks of the participant's degree of social conformity before and after the experimentation, and if any differences should exist within these two domains. The basis of these questions is to assist in the follow-up study to determine any effects the experiment would possess on its participants (Asch, 1955).

Conclusion. In following-up the study, the best conclusion to derive from test results would be through the occurrence of individual contact with test members. Survey questions can act as a means of measuring if the results would meet expectations, and if the study, in fact would possess any long-term results on decision-making. One may make the assumption not all study members to be affected in the same manner. The study results itself would demonstrate this, 25% would respond 100% correct, 63% of the responses would be correct, among other statistics demonstrating differential affect (Asch, 1955, p. 3). The peculiarity of the Asch study would not take from its effectiveness in supporting earlier conclusions basing upon social psychology research.

Psychology in Action Part VIII

Solomon E Asch Follow-up Inventory

1. What are your major reasons for conforming?

Dependence on the group
Feelings of inadequacy
Felt it was the right thing to do
Remained independent

2. What are your reasons for remaining independent?

I do not care what others think
I know I am right
It seemed like the right thing to do
I conformed

3. How would you best describe yourself after taking part in the experiment?

As a perfectionist
Sensitive to criticism
Unstable
Attention seeking

4. Which aspect of your personality would affect your decision-making during the experimentation?

My lack of care for others
My Instability
My need for admiration
My detachment from normal social relations

5. Which statement best describes you?

I really couldn't care any less of the happiness of others
I just want to be taken care of
A job isn't done until it's done right
Your threatening me and I do not trust you

6. If you were to conform to the test what would be the reasons?

My need to be nurtured
My feelings of inadequacy
Just seemed like the thing to do at the time
I did conform

7. If you were to remain independent during the test what would be the reason?

My preoccupation with perfection
I don't care about the happiness of others
Just seemed like the thing to do at the time
I did remain independent

8. Which statement least describes you.
I am a caring person
I am not perfect
No one takes care of me except for me
I am a self-confident person

9. Typically people describe me as

A perfectionist
Detached from the social environment
Uncomfortable in social situations

Unconfident

10. Why didn't you just the answer the question as you would have otherwise?

Felt I would be more taken care of by conforming to the group
Insecurities
I don't know
I did I remained independent throughout

Solomon E Asch Follow-up Inventory (Link)
http://www.surveymonkey.com/s/RPHBVZR

Personality Assessment Tool Evaluation

Personality Assessment Tool Evaluation involves responding to a personality assessment instruments chart. Upon the completion of the chart the selection of six instruments of personality measurement would meet selection, including the NEO PI-R, "thematic apperception test" (TAT), "locus of control" scale, multi-motive grid, Rorschach inkblot test, and the Minnesota multiphasic personality inventory (MMPI). Among these inventories various elements would be a topic of selection, including reliability, validity, unity and cultural fairness, theoretical foundation, and the pros and cons of the instrument of selection. In selection of one assessment method over another the means may be individual knowledge. Despite individual variables, test variables may require the use of one test over another within different situations.

NEO PI-R - Paul T. Costa, Jr., PhD and Robert R. McCrae, PhD. The neuroticism-extroversion-openness inventory (NEO PI-R) would develop in 1990 by Paul T. Costa, Jr., PhD and Robert R. McCrae, PhD. This would act as a revision to the earlier version in 1978 as the NEO P-I. The theoretical foundation of the NEO PI-R bases on the five factor theory. Positives of the NEO PI-R are its usefulness in measuring personality traits and the basic tendencies and characteristic adaptations of the individual (McCrae & Costa, 2003). A weakness of the NEO PI-R is it lacks cultural fairness requiring the use of language to accomplish the test. The NEO PI-R would need to be in different languages to accommodate this weakness. Despite contending theories disputing the number of present personality dispositions, the inventory would continue to be an accurate measure of personality traits of which it designs. The testing would seem consistent across the duration of the test. A possible weakness is the prospect of continuity in consideration to reliability.

Thematic Apperception Test (TAT) - Henry Murray and Christiana Morgan. The development of the "thematic apperception test" (TAT) would be a product of the work of Henry Murray and Christian Morgan in 1935 (Larsen & Buss, 2010, p. 336). The test bases on Henry Murray's theory of needs. The strength of the test is as a measure of momentary need. Another strength is the cultural fairness to the test, which does not require the same use of language as a self-report test. Though apparently less complicated, the TAT would seem devoid of the same weaknesses of other tests. The validity of the test may be a determinant of the tester/experimenter who interprets the results. The scorer possesses the same task in creating a consistent examination.

Locus of Control Scale - Julian Rotter. The locus of control scale would be a product of Julian Rotter in 1966 (Feist & Feist, 2009). The basis to the locus of control scale would appear to apply to the cognitive social learning theory a product of Rotter and Walter Mischel. The strength of the scale is its ability to measure the level of control one possesses over his or her life (Larsen & Buss, 2010, p. 661). The use of language within the test would create a nonculturally fair examination. The validity for this reason would not pertain to one speaking a foreign language. The test does seem to measure accurately the domain it intends in locus of control. The test is consistent over the testing process.

Multi-motive Grid - H. D. Schmalt. The multi-motive grid is a product of H. D. Schmalt created in 1976 (Larsen & Buss, 2010, p. 337). The multi-motive grid seems to be pertinent to McClelland's achievement motivation theory. A strength of the multi-motive grid is its ability to measure motivation and achievement. The test combines both aspects of projective tests and self-reports. This can act as both a strength and weakness as the more elaborate test diminishes cultural fairness. The aim of the test is met as a measure of achievement and motivation, and the test appears consistent with the experimenter playing a factor. The continuity of the test is an issue.

Rorschach Inkblot Test - Herman Rorschach. Herman Rorschach in 1921 would be the original creator of the Rorschach inkblot test (Larsen & Buss, 2010, p. 34). The test would go through improvements with the addition of the Exner scoring system by John Exner. The Rorschach test theory would act as the basis of the test. The strength of the Rorschach is in its ability to assess personality. As a projective technique the test is more culturally fair than other inventories, especially the self-reporting variety. The Exner scoring system would make the test a more accurate measure of personality. Consistency may be an issue as one may see a different image in the inkblot even a short time later.

Minnesota Multiphasic Personality Inventory (MMPI) - J. C. McKinley and S. R. Hathaway. The construction of the Minnesota Multiphasic Personality Inventory (MMPI) would occur in 1939 through the work of J. C. McKinley and S. R. Hathaway. The inventory would base upon a Gordon Allport theory, psychology of the individual theory. The usefulness of the MMPI is as a screening process for potential officers. The inventory consists of 550 questions detecting significant psychological problems (Larsen & Buss, 2010, p. 116). The test unless offered in different languages would not represent a culturally fair inventory. A possible weakness among other self-reports is the individual may respond untruthfully to hide relevant information. Despite this, as a measure of mental health is mostly accurate. A demonstration of test consistency occurs through its use as a screening process among potential officers (Larsen & Buss, 2010, p. 116).

Conclusion. Each inventory possesses their own set of strengths and weaknesses. A common element among the various inventories is an ignorance in the cultural fairness of an inventory. This is the result of the added importance of language within the testing procedure. Such tests are often more complicated and can be useful to hire employees or screen government officials (MMPI). These tests may gain strengths in the weakness of cultural fairness. Culturally fair inventories are often through projective techniques displaying personality characteristics without the major use of language. In consideration of test reliability and validity, one may make better decisions in which type of test to administer upon an individual or group.

Appendix

Personality Assessment Instruments (Link).
https://skydrive.live.com/redir?page=view&resid=CE8CE8CBC7AFDC84!1338&authkey=!ALOl_5nnXVVY5ig

Psychology in Action Part IX

Implications of Asch Study

Researcher's Interpretation of Personality Related Behaviors. The focus of the Solomon E Asch study as the study name would imply (Opinions and Social Pressure) is on the effect of social pressures on individual opinion. The implication the research or researcher Solomon Asch in this case would make is personality and the behaviors pertaining to personality are in large part a construction of social influence. Asch would demonstrate individual's responses to vary basing upon the response of a group. In this sense the measure of personality would base upon responses to the social climate. Personality behaviors, according to Asch can modify greatly through contact from a majority group of three to 15 who each are responding erroneously. The result in such a scenario is a 36.8% error response rate compared to a margin of error of less than 1% (Asch, 1955, p. 3). Among this error rate and the respondent population of 123 participants, only 25% would never agree with the deceitful and erroneous majority group. This would show despite a 36.8% error rate an increase of over 35% more errors, 75% of the respondents would demonstrate an altering of personality related behaviors on account of the social setting (Asch, 1955, p. 4). Asch further demonstrates how personality behaviors fluctuate basing upon the social setting. When the individual should have a partner answering correctly among this social setting the error response rate would drop to 25%. With a group of two dissenters in the social setting the error rate would drop to 13.6%, and one person in the social setting responding incorrectly would possess no effect on the rate of error. Further demonstrating the implications of Asch in personality related behavior to be a product of the social setting is the partner of the participant responding more incorrectly than the group, the error rate diminishes to 9%

comparing to 21.5% in the opposite scenario. A partner abandoning to the dissenting group would result in an error rate returning to the 36.8% of the normal wrongful majority group response (Asch, 1955, p. 5). It would seem Asch's implication personality related behavior to be a product and influenced by the social setting to prove correct in a decisive manner.

Implications of Asch Study for Interpreting Behavior

Employment. Asch would imply behavior in the employment environment to vary basing on one's surroundings. Some individuals only work with coworkers and others customers and coworkers. The manner in which the individual behaves in the employment arena may be an evolutionary process of witnessing the behaviors of other coworkers in his or her fashion of working and dealing with customers. It would seem norms to form in this fashion through a socialization process. The employment rules may be part of the socialization process catering to production. In the employment arena one may receive influence more from tacit knowledge employees or high paying customers. As the majority of workers conform to a norm, the norm acts as the majority influence, which as Asch implies account for personality or personality related behaviors.

Social. In the social setting Asch assumes the individual would conform to the crowd better to fit in. The consensus, according to the Asch study is conforming to the group is more compatible. This demonstration is visible through the fact 75% of respondents among his demonstration would alter responses basing upon the group's response, despite the error rate only as high as 36.8% among the large unanimous group of dissenters. Asch would assume 25% of individuals not to be as conforming to the social setting (Asch, 1955, pp. 4, 5). Such a personality disposition may function well among the social setting. In both cases the social setting is affecting decision-making and in more cases than not personality behaviors are catering to the social environment.

Personal. The personal setting of the individual is just this and can range among the other settings. Personal behavior is a decision, and in consideration of motivation is to attain a goal in the release of tension. The conforming individual is doing so in the attempt of alleviating tension. Apparently large groups of people with different views create a greater amount of tension and result in a greater deal of conformity. Asch may not be able to determine why some are more likely and others less likely to conform. These are personal behaviors and can divulge information of the individual. Asch determines the personal behaviors among most alter opinion and greatly affect decision-making.

Research. Asch's study would be a demonstration of behavior in the research setting. The research would measure the rate behavior would alter among the social setting upon manipulation of the social setting. The individual does know he is part of research, yet would not be aware he would be the focal subject. The subjects' behavior in the research setting, one may assume would transfer to each the other settings of personal, social, and employment.

Psychology in Action Part X

Impact of Asch Study on the Treatment of Personality Disorder

Contribution of Social Settings to Disorder. The Asch study impacts the study of personality disorders from the perspective of the social setting as a contributor to the disorder. As an example one may view independence as forms of anti-sociality or obsessive compulsion. Conversely one's need to conform, according to Asch may associate with an avoidant or dependent personality. Anti-socials describe as psychopathic caring little of the happiness of others. Such individuals do not care what others are doing accounting for their independent nature. The preoccupation for perfection among obsessive compulsives can lead to their independence knowing they are right and will not stray for anyone (Larsen & Buss, 2010, p. 614). The feelings of inadequacy among avoidant personality disorder can cause conforming just as the need to receive nurturance among dependent personality disorder can lead to their conforming personality. The Asch study can divulge much information pertinent to personality disorder should one possess an understanding of the traits associating with the disorders.

Asch Follow-up Study Offers Insight into Treatment of Personality Disorders

Erratic, Eccentric, and Anxious Clusters. In applying Asch's study and how it may pertain to personality disorder, upon a follow-up study it may be possible to make any connections among the participants to possible traits compatible with the various personality disorders. A personality disorder is a behavioral pattern or experience painful or distressing to an individual associating with increased risk of death, confinement, or loss of function, and leads to impairment in important life domains or could lead to disability.

The study of personality disorder would occur within abnormal psychology, abnormal as simply anything straying from the norm. In existence are 10 types of personality disorders falling into a triadic taxonomy of erratic, eccentric, and anxious clusters (Larsen & Buss, 2010, p. 584). The antisocial person is a sociopath or psychopath and such a person cares very little of the happiness of others. Perhaps Asch may state independent individuals to display more a tendency toward antisocial personality disorder. In another sense a participant after such an experiment, one may argue could develop traits associating with antisocial personality disorder paying less mind to the opinions of one's social setting. Instability is the mark of borderline personality disorder as everything in the individual's life can be unstable from self-image, to behavior, to emotions, and finally to relationships (p. 597). An unstable self-image may gravitate further into instability through participation in the Asch study. One may create false perceptions of persecution. Asch may suggest such an individual not to adapt well to his or her surroundings. Excessive attention seeking and emotionality are the traits of histrionic personality disorder. If an individual enjoys attention, a participant of this opinion and social pressure experiment is certainly his or her environment (p. 600). Despite the nature of the examination as non-therapeutic, it will cater certainly to their personality. The symptoms of narcissistic personality are a lack of insight into the feelings of others, a strong sense of importance, and the need for admiration. Once again the Asch study would be a fitting environment for such an individual. It would seem in a social setting such an individual would possess the desire to be the center of attention finding him or herself of more importance than others. This may be the factor to treat in crediting others for their achievements as well.

The eccentric cluster consists of three personality disorders: paranoid personality disorder, schizoid personality disorder, and schizotypal personality disorder (p. 604). The individual of a schizoid personality detaches from normal social relations. Perhaps Asch would state within the social setting for the individual to possess of some sort of conflict among demonstrating independence of conforming to a group. This clash it is possible may contribute to such schisms among the personality. The primary component of schizotypal personality disorder are sharp feelings of discomfort in social relationships. Such an individual may not be capable of handling an all verse one feeling and as acute discomfort presents itself so too does the schizotypal personality. The defining feature of paranoid personality disorder is the view of others as a threat leading to severe feelings of distrust. The individual who views group opinion as a threat may develop distrust for a group. It is this distrust from lack of coping skills contributing to paranoid personality disorder according to Asch.

The final cluster the anxious cluster includes avoidant personality disorder, dependent personality disorder, and obsessive-compulsive personality disorder (p. 610). The defining feature of avoidant personality disorder is a sensitivity to the criticism of others or feelings of inadequacy. The feelings of inadequacy may within the study cause one to conform in avoidance of criticism for their independence. The defining features of dependent personality disorder is an excessive need for nurturance or taken care of. Just as the avoidant personality may conform so too will the dependent personality but for different reasons. Such an individual may conform to experience nurturance by the large group. The defining features of obsessive-compulsive personality disorder include a striving to be perfect and a preoccupation to be perfect. Such an individual, unlike others of the anxious cluster may remain independent in his or her quest for perfection.

References

Asch, S. E. (1955). *Opinions and social pressure. Scientific American, 193*(5), 31-35. Retrieved April 30, 2008, from http://www.columbia.edu/cu/psychology/terrace/w1001/readings/asch.pdf

Bass, B.M. and Avolio, BJ. (1993). Transformational leadership: A response to critiques. *Leadership Theory and Research: Perspectives and Directions*, 49-80. Academic Press, San Diego, CA.

Bernstein, D. A, Penner, L. A., Clarke-Stewart, A., Roy, E. J. (2012). *Psychology*. (9th ed). Wadsworth, Cengage Learning.

Cherry, K. (2013). Solomon Asch biography. *About.com. Psychology*. Retrieved from http://psychology.about.com/od/profilesal/p/solomon-asch.htm

Cloninger, S. C. (2008). *Theories of personality: Understanding persons* (5th ed.). Upper Saddle River, NJ: Pearson Prentice Hall.

Corner, R. J. (2005). *Fundamentals of abnormal psychology* (4th ed.). New York: Worth.

Dambrun, M., & Vatiné, E. (2010). Reopening the study of extreme social behaviors: Obedience to authority within an immersive video environment. *European Journal Of Social Psychology, 40*(5), 760-773.

DuBoff, R. (1989). *Accumulation & power*. Armonke, NY. M.E. Sharpe.

Hodges, B. H. (2004). Asch and the balance of values. *Behavioral and Brain Sciences, 27*(3), 343-344.

Kenrick, D. T., Neuberg, S. L., & Cialdini, R. B. (2010). *Social psychology: Goals in interaction* (5th ed.). Boston, MA: Pearson.

Larsen, R. J., & Buss, D. M. (2010). *Personality psychology: Domains of knowledge about human nature* (4th ed.). Boston, MA: McGraw-Hill.

Lawson, R. B., Graham, J. E., & Baker, K. M. (2007). *A history of psychology: Globalization, ideas, and applications*. Published by Prentice Hall.

Milgram, S. (1964). Group pressure and action against a person. *The Journal of Abnormal and Social Psychology, 69*(2), 137.

Myers, D. (2010). *Social Psychology* (10th ed.). New York: McGraw Hill.

Santee, R. T. & Maslach, C. (1982). To agree or not to agree: Personal dissent amid social pressure to conform. *Journal of Personality and Social Psychology, 42*(4), 690-700. doi: 10.1037/0022-3514.42.4.690

Spector, P. E. (2008). *Industrial and organizational psychology: Research and practice* (5th ed.). Hoboken, NJ: Wiley.

Uniformed Code of Military Justice. (2013). *Article 92*. Retrieved from http://www.au.af.mil/au/awc/awcgate/ucmj.htm#SUB CHAPTER 1. GENERAL PROVISIONS

Made in the USA
Monee, IL
13 October 2020

44934373R00039